Management Poems by Madhoo

Competition

Main Poem

Competition is a game with market players,

Few leaders and some swayers,

Some giants and many a small one,

Companies to beat market, some in groups as if already won,

Marching on financial statements,

Harping on products and consignments,

Haggling with vendors and many a client,

To get denials and make some compliant,

Counting on the customers,

Some old and some first timers,

Reading on to the bourses,

Numbers on magical courses,

Dealing with issues,

Governments in various hues,

Employments as some for hires,

Promoting, demoting and some fires,

Comparing with competitors,

Failing as repeaters,

Still firms form, survive, grow and compete,

The industry phases somehow repeat.

Cascading Poems

The following remaining poems cascade from the main poem.

Competition is a game with market players

Some monopolists, others oligopolists,

Some naysayers, some followers,

Some leaders, some laggards,

The market has others too,

Not any other but the customers,

Who are our own,

Their needs are our business,

Their orders are our profits,

We need them, and they need us,

Compete to get to the best.

For market is not without them,

They are the players because they create the market in helm,

Other players cannot play,

If not for customers on the way,

To smile and give companies some rules of the game.

Few leaders and some swayers

Naysayers turn into swayers,

And create slowdowns and crises,

Leaders form their markets,

Leaders create histories,

Out of loyal customers and new ways,

Leaders make over decades,

With patience when they serve nations,

Leaders make their own industries,

With barriers for entry and exits,

Leaders grow into giants,

With markets, customers and adherents.

Swayers fail to doom,

When they refuse to bloom,

With stale products one too many defective,

Didn't we see DEC or Lehman,

But we also see Wal-Mart and Citibank.

Some giants and many a small one

We revel, say competitors many or one,

It's all in the game,

Whether big or small in name,

Giants compete on size,

Minis compete on quality,

Giants take to floor markets,

Minis fly to soaring sockets,

Smalls have customers, beyond a count,

Giants have funds, beyond a limit,

Regulators are mothers and fathers,

For they know no difference between giants or smalls,

Ground is open for all,

These are not to say that the rest is forbidden lot.

Companies to beat market, some in groups as if already won

Market has all but not one,

Groups that are sometimes strategic or clusters,

Victory that is beforehand won,

Some that strive on own,

Partners, alliances or ventures in joint or acquisitions,

Industries that try to beat market expectations,

At times, the ruthless market that shakes the spine,

Gets the chill down its spine.

When customers welcome companies,

But deadbeat in the industries,

Nobody can understand the markets,

So can't the customers,

Philosophy of competition is humongous,

Endless, trails full on rails, and some bogus,

Consistent ones win whether alone
or together,

For that is the market unity with
all,

Regulators, buyers and sellers.

Marching on financial statements

Well, who said companies don't look at profits,

Making money is the goal of all parties,

All compete, for social tag too,

They serve the community interests,

But cry when profits see reds,

The income statement makes all nervous,

Companies are no less frivolous,

Then losses get heavy,

When firms lose sight,

Of finances, investments and returns,

They say don't compete in blinds,

See the funds and tights,

See the flows – ins and outs,

Sum the assets, deduct the liabilities,

With the ratios, Maths is in its heights,

Use everything for success,

Or else failure will use it all,

Success and failure compete too.

Harping on products and consignments

Vendors, suppliers, channels, partners,

And many more that tell where to harvest,

HP, Dell and IBM compete on PCs,

Microsoft, Sun, and Android compete on packages,

Kraft-Cadbury, Nestle and Parle compete on chocolates,

Cookies, shapes, sizes and colors,

For they make each a different product.

Dealers, stores, distributors, compete on supplies,

Each wants the best consignments,

On time, cost and quality to best selects,

Avail that are put to buyers,

In rebates, discounts, coupons and vouchers,

Some on order processing, some on delivery times,

Some on packaging, some on warranting deals.

Damages and defectives,
        replacements, returns,

Exchanges, losses with no care to
        watchers,

Those that don't buy, those that
        are not loyal,

But still compete for them all,

For companies never know who
        will save their mile.

Haggling with vendors and many a client

Tenders, bids, negotiations, prices with least decimals in difference,

Vendors that hail to glory for the clients,

Or that they will be the ones for life,

Taking on different hats, once a vendor, once a client,

Companies have no go, except to serve customers,

To save their logo, and make monies,

For customers also haggle,

Sometimes deal that is in middle,

So many to negotiate, tiring at times,

Exciting to taste, goals are not many,

But one to make money,

Means are many and may be ends so many,

Still it is the best in the lot to win,

That competes against all odds in the wind,

Storm in the cup, that passes the company,

If fought with rigor, companies can win all negotiations.

To get denials and make some compliant

Many players in the lot make the playground so hot,

Blazing with speed are the buyers,

With demands always on the top tiers,

They say yes, yet no to the same product on shelves,

Running for business and deals,

Are the suppliers, or vendors to meet needs,

They find a deal, yet no deal for many years,

Nobody knows how market thinks,

Sometimes as cruel and at times at well,

Welfare and doom for companies that sell,

Amidst all refusals, no, denials, and admirers,

Some of those knock, as opportunity or shock,

Some that rock as hits or sharps,

Agreements that end without a dime,

Others that last through a decade like a rhyme,

Competition is between denials and acceptance,

For companies that know no way but to dance,

To the tunes of markets and buyers,

To make green monies or else be dryers.

Counting on the customers

The customers that agree to be with thee for life,

Often shift sides without a rife,

Markets do not question customers,

For customers are the Gods of the competitors,

Support is needed from all corners,

In making them happy, one and all adorners,

For they make or break,

Companies those are not awake,

Markets are created by customers,

With sellers, makers, companies, manufacturers,

That spread to nations to get foreign advantages,

Customers give the motivation to innovate,

Whether it is Honda, Germany or Bill Gates,

Customers can create companies,

Customers can create advantages on locations,

Customers can make a king-maker in business.

Count on the customers, but never discount them.

Some old and some first timers

In the game, rules are always timers,

Whether the players are new or old,

All need to side by the rules.

In the competition, strategy is always a game,

Whether new or old,

All need to own one.

Resources are inputs for all,

Whether new or old in the game,

They need to compete on all.

Markets don't forgive always,

If limping young or laming old,

When sun shines, Companies all need to make hays.

Customers think at times,

And go with the old timers,

But just for dimes.

Buyers then jump at gun,

And rest on new one,

The fledgling has won.

Source the best, sell the better of the best.

Reading on to the bourses

Markets cry and laugh,

Companies smile and weep,

When stocks rise and sweep,

When exchanges yield and ruin,

As if the report cards with monitors,

Companies that scroll on to their losses,

Gains that make investors,

Or break trust with sellers,

Bourses hang onto the stock symbols,

Counters tick onto the minute changes,

Buyers and sellers that trade in the scrip,

Sometimes at highs and at others lows,

Some ranking high, some on the red,

Greens that pass, with distinction,

As dividends or silence,

To investors that wait and watch,

Some those buy, sell or hold,

Some that abandon if not bold.

Numbers on magical courses

Numbers and Maths are never dead,

For they see companies in rise and red,

If not in profits, losses, to earn and pay,

In assets, balances, to invest and wait,

In donations or capitals that earn a name,

Goodwill in numbers of followers,

Well-wishers Of companies,

In buyers, investors and promoters,

Ambassadors, brokers, agents, dealers,

Those create magic in numbers,

Sometimes in revenues, others in volumes,

At times in segments, customers and markets,

To rule the domestic or global as martinets,

Upswing or downswing, troughs or crests,

Candles or butterflies, risks or limits,

These numbers make the destinies of companies,

Those compete constantly without count of concern any.

Dealing with issues

Does it all end with business,

That is an ocean of joys and concerns,

Issues of vendors boggling in doubts,

Issues of buyers haggling in counts,

Issues of governments struggling in documents,

Issues of sectors dominating in strategies,

Issues of industries lagging in monies,

Issues of strategic groups lost in tactics,

Issues of competitors jumping for yardsticks,

Issues of new players wrestling against benchmarks,

Issues of failures and crises,

Issues of exits and reestablishments,

Issues of quality and labor unrests,

Issues of unions and reunions,

Issues of mergers and acquisitions,

Issues of locations and capabilities,

Issues of diamonds and competitive advantages,

Companies compete for comparative advantage, local and global.

Governments in various hues

Regulators that wrench the firms,

With rule that hangs or mimes,

Jingles with companies and
employees,

Create groups and divisions among
top and rung,

Resistance and inertia in some or
all,

Support that is converted for none,

Unless there is a carrot,

Often as a tarot,

Deadlines that beat to blues,

Headlines that stutter to hues,

Defaulters that break into rules,

Government as father of naughty,

Firms those become haughty,

Like the Enron or Satyam,

Government show the stick,

And make the competition tick.

Employments as some for hires

Companies compete but
sometimes defeat,

When they hire and fire,

Employees on contract or ever,

Benefits as that may last or be lost,

Retirements that may be secure or
haywire,

Others prove satisfaction, some
attain it,

Employees in good companies or
not,

Not unknown that Dell hires if IBM
fires,

Such is the competition that,

Google hires Yahoo CEO,

Or gaming with the ecology,

Making downsizing impacts on economy,

Dictate the rules as competing with roles,

In delegating as if in the making,

Firms that lose on competition,

Try to gain on employment,

For happy employees are the ways to satisfied customers.

Promoting, demoting and some fires

Customers are not less ruthless,

When clients go against the employees,

For reasons major or trivial,

Promotions on the hilt,

When clients give in their applause,

Perks on the halt, otherwise,

Projects on the roll, products on the sale,

When employees do their best with buyers,

When employees do their best with bosses,

When employees do their best with peers,

When employees do their best with subordinates,

Or else love turns into hatreds,

Ladder turns into slide,

Career turns into forest fire,

Competition may admire,

For they may even hire some in ire,

To sprinkle water on the spot,

And make their rolls shinier,

Those qualified and skilled,

Those experts and drilled,

Can make it on any desk,

So long as official and competing.

Comparing with competitors

Faring and comparing, is not unheard of,

In the raring and daring, business as a role,

Competitors as participants, in the network,

That is sometimes loose, and may be close,

At times open and tight, to wind up all,

Racing against each other's nose,

Piping with customers new and old,

Tipping with losses, spreads and margins,

Roaring in employees, working and slogging,

Rating with agencies berating or soaring,

Gaming with nations, location and resources,

Impressing regulators, hard and light,

Complying with seasons, costly and forced,

Gambling with fortunes, efficiency, productivity, savings,

Winning and losing as early-mover or follower or exits,

Reducing on waste, recycling, and green,

Companies in haste or late,

Some as winners, some as averages, some as losers,

Some as gamblers, some as planners, and some emerge as strategists.

Failing as repeaters

Companies that innovate, win the road to hail,

Those that follow set a path on the wait,

Those that create but customers berate,

Fail because of the mistakes they repeat,

In the hands of channels, failures fail to cooperate,

In the ground of competitors, failures fail to collaborate,

Not once but many times in runs,

Racing at pace lagging markets,

They fail or else ruin the markets,

When several failures repeat,

Industry takes the beat,

Still repeats run in the race,

Economy takes the heat,

Falters the race itself,

Then the crisis recurs,

Warnings that get ignored,

Alerts that get unanswered,

Rest in the base of the economy,

And make it rancid,

For all competitors with no go but be placid.

Still firms form, survive, grow and compete

Competition is endless, the saga goes on,

Old ones die, new ones shine, giants grow,

New ones fizzle, old ones dazzle, small ones form,

Industry invades, cycles form, phases change,

Firms dominate, compete and lead,

Others that need help, support and heed,

Bail out as they will be,

By competition or government,

Economies care for industries,

Industries care for companies,

Companies care for customers,

Customers care for technologies,

Technologies care for nations,

Nations care for globalization,

And vice versa, because,

All care for environmental improvement,

Consultants and scholars,

Corporates and customers,

Every time the world is in
transition.

The industry phases somehow repeat

Dumping, wastes, unskilled labor,

Repeat with industry success and glamour,

We need to harvest the crop,

By protecting it from weeds,

If not always, we learn to adapt the seeds,

So are companies that come with their own,

Strengths and weaknesses, that industries adopt,

A phase that is a boom, another that is a doom,

A phase that is in growth, another that is stagnant,

A phase that is mature, another that is nascent,

Companies that straddle between phases,

Learning and experience grows and determines,

Creating new competitive models,

Not-for-profit and revenue marchers,

Integrating industries in backward and in soar,

Like HMO, McDonalds, or Ford,

Health, Insurance and Dynamic reforms,

It's our world and world's business,

That needs to grow and flourish.

Madhoo is a Doctor of Philosophy in Strategic Management. The poetic style adopted in this anthology is that of Cascading poems.

www.ingramcontent.com/pod-product-compliance
Lightning Source LLC
Chambersburg PA
CBHW071643170526
45166CB00003B/1409